Test Swan

Poems by J.I.B.

Columbus, Ohio
empbooks.com

Back-Pocket Edition: 10 19 33 34 6 11 1973
ISBN: 979-8-88596-195-0
LOC:2023931775
Design, Layout, and Edits: Ezhno Martín
Cover Art: Travis Neil Herman

— To everyone who's ever plucked
a feather off my body,
and to everyone who's lent it one.

Smothered

He heard somebody telling somebody else about some woman in New Boston who smothered her baby. He knew *smothered* was bad because the person telling looked sour and the person listening frowned and shook her head. But he thought *smothered* sounded pretty and soft like *pillow* or *blanket*. He asked his mother what it meant. She asked him why he wanted to know. So he told her about how the person told the other person about the woman in New Boston who smothered her baby. She told him that smothering was a bad thing that makes it so you can't breathe. He knew that if you don't breathe you die. Surely nobody would want to make a baby dead. Old people die and people get sad but it's okay because they're old and they've had time. Babies are new and need time to get old. He never saw a dead person before. Besides on TV. But that isn't real. Those are actors and they die a lot and have all kinds of different names. He thought maybe the woman in New Boston didn't know that smothering was a bad thing because it's such a soft word.

1

The Anatomy of Angels
and Their Dysfunction

As beautiful as they look in renaissance
paintings   the bodies of angels are ugly
miracles. With every flight   they cause
internal damage   the likes of which can
never be repaired   or even scab over.
Every time a wing flaps   it saws away at
its shoulder blades. This   wound   makes
it impossible   to fly as high as they did
the last time. When their   arms finally pop
off like strip mall mannequins   when they
take the form of Venus   fall to Earth
from their latest low point   they often
ask God why   He made something just for
it to malfunction.   Why He gave them the
desire to soar   just to have it   ruin
them.

The Book of Genesis,
as Interpreted by J.I.B.

God shattered Himself on the second day of
construction (second only to the invention
of light). This is where we inherit
destruction. By the sixth day   man was
cutting his feet. God said this was   good.
Instructed them to seek repair / to learn
to pray for it.   Said these wounds are a
test.   This life is but vapor.   Something
about the merit of free will.   By the
seventh day   man was wearing sandals.

The Three Wives of Adam

Praiseless   and with all the wrath His
body could muster   God drove His bare
hands into the torso of the Earth   freshly
constructed   and skinless   and from
its dirt   and its rocks   and its dust
made Adam   a drooling hulking form. Like
a confused child   screaming for comfort
Adam demanded something living   and soft
to suckle at. So God dug into Adam's body
as brutally as he could   unwilling to
leave anything whole   ripped out a set
a ribs   and got to work. His first wife
built to be durable enough to withstand
constant bending and molding   but too
fragile to fight back   simply refused to
be eaten by something so desperate   and
so savage. With great pleasure and labor
and with bullets of sweat bleeding from
His brow   God made waste of her womb
casted her out   armless   made her
crawl through the wilderness on her naked
chest and belly. After the removal of more
bones   God tried again   only this
time He showed Adam the hideous process of
transfiguring calcium into a human being.
Disgusted by this display   this

oozing thing   without flesh   Adam
raged   battered her with white knuckles
and stone. She ran away   incomplete   and
wounded. Like a confused child   screaming
for comfort   Adam would have killed God
had he only had the strength. By the time
his third wife was formed   Adam   nearly
boneless   could no longer stand on his
own two feet   but he finally stopped
screaming   opened his mouth wide
stuck out his tongue.

It's a Miracle We're Not All Covered in Blood Pt. 1

The first human body was made of clipped
feathers   attached to a skeleton of
wax. It was fruitful and multiplied. The
boys were fed plates of gunpowder / were
turned into AK47s. Divine intervention
made porcelain of the girls. They were
given   instructions   on   how   to   mold
themselves/ how to fill   the   resulting
cracks.   Told to dance   until they no
longer   had   ankles. Eventually the
ground   was paved   with their shards.

The Story of Noah and the Ark,
as Interpreted by J.I.B.

In one of His rages   God drowned
the whole planet in   His bath water.
Said   *Look at what you made me do.*
Said   *This is the only way to get you clean.*
Said   *This is an act of love.*
After all   He left the obedient to float like
rubber ducks. Like all toxic relationships
love was confused with mercy   and wrath
considered a byproduct of intimacy. As is
the occasional impulse to   dismantle
everything   you've created.   To start
from scratch. To promise to rebuild. To
never destroy   the same way again.

The Tree of Life in Metric Tons

The   conception of Christ   wasn't
painless. God was not gentle. A miracle.
The formation of a skeleton strong enough
to carry the weight   of the   Tree of Life
in its entirety. A skull made to bear a
crown   of thorns. No. This   like the
forgiveness of sin   requires bloodshed
will leave a mark.   Make no mistake
Christ is not beautiful   in Heaven.
He bares every little wound. He did not
crawl out   of the tomb   float towards
Seraphim effortlessly   and without wings.
He was   dragged   bleeding   having
saved   no one. No. The conception
of Christ was not painless. God refused to
be gentle.   A sacrifice. This   like the
forgiveness of sin   required bloodshed
for some reason.

It's a Miracle We're All Not Covered in Blood   Pt. 2

Somewhere inside the human torso   most
likely buried beneath the rib cage   is
an empty box. This is where God   is
supposed to live. Like human beings   God
creates   without much concern for the
resulting victims. This   box is not the
work of a skilled craftsman. A splintered
jagged contraption   decorated in rust and
plucked thorns. It succeeded only in being
big enough.   Like God   human beings
have a need to fill   in their
voids. Presented with the absence of   God
we eat handfuls. Whatever we can find.   We
rip our bodies nearly to pieces   ignoring
the   bleeding.   We stretch our throats
our mouths   beyond the limits of their
design   while somewhere in the known and
useless universe   God is creating   more

empty

space.

The Gospel of Jesus Christ Failing

I am certain that currently no one is being saved. This is because we don't have a protagonist that we can see ourselves in. This isn't a new idea. Imagine Christ strung out. Or dope sick. Hopeless. In a robe of piss. In a fit of rage. In the desert. Maybe bloodmouthed. Maybe cracktoothed. Maybe with a tongue of sand and pebbles having just bitten into bread that then instantly turned back into stone. With a woman inside him like leprosy. Imagine Christ screaming. Maybe at his bastard child. Or hating his own mother. Imagine Christ Godless. Or during another night of disappointing his lover. Imagine if he told us that nothing he does is miraculous but rather the result of great effort and strain. Imagine Christ making his grandmother mourn a grandson she no longer recognizes. Imagine Christ wishing he were good. Imagine Christ on a cross. Resurrecting without saving anyone. Imagine Christ not just flying off to Heaven effortlessly and without wings but staying. Trying again. This isn't a new idea. We need our protagonist to learn something.

Why Infants Cry

They have an innate understanding of the
mathematics of loss and being.   That the
constant addition   and subtraction of our
parts is natural.   This is instinctual.
Most   things   are   learned   behaviors
like fearing God.   Pretending to
be a ghost. Or   most importantly   how
to wake up every morning   how to bury
the infant in your torso   tuck it under
your lungs. At night   it crawls back out
screaming   for fresh air.

Sink or Swim

Sometimes when newborns aren't held enough
they   stop breathing.   I theorize
this is because   they start to hate the
taste of air after a while.   They leave
in search for a sweeter atmosphere. The
only things we know from birth is how to
breathe and consume.   Neither of these
drives are ever satisfied. This is because
God left Eden prematurely never finished
breast feeding.   Now the human ghost is
hungry   deformed   shaped like a
leaking sink   a clogged drain   on
the verge overflowing. On second thought
maybe it isn't the taste of air. Maybe
they leave to keep from drowning   unable
to keep their heads above water   without
a helping hand.

The Three Baptisms of J.I.B.

There's a parable about a drunken preacher
who once didn't stop a baptism until the
bubbles stopped. The river was green and
cold   and   at first   the body was warm
and the fish wouldn't swim near it. This
parable can be quickly transformed into a
joke   the preacher   after seeing what a
mess he made   rejoiced. *It was God's will
that the boy was drowned.* I won't make a
tired observation about God's cruel sense
of humor.   I'll just remind you that
Christ told his followers   12 unmarried men
who would die   alienated and very
painfully   that it is no good for man to
be alone.   The parable becomes an urban
legend   the preacher was forgiven and the
boy was never pulled from the water   and
once the body was cold   the fish began
to eat it   until it was gone. The first
time I was baptized   I was a child no one
would swim near. I thought that   maybe
it was because I wasn't clean. Some people
will tell you the parable isn't a parable
but a true story.   That the drunken
preacher didn't   accidentally   drown
a boy   during a baptism.   He did it in
a bathtub   and it was his son   and it
wasn't a   baptism   or an accident.

In court   he said it was just like
when God asked Abrham to kill his first
born   only this time   God forgot   to
have him stop.   The second time I was
baptized   I was terrified   certain my
body had been eaten   almost entirely.
The parable   would have been a fable
had the fish just opened their mouths   and
spoke up. The third time   I don't think
I had ever had a body at all.   I was
told to be patient   was reminded that God
once demanded   his most obedient servant
marry a lustful woman who could never love
him. Some people will tell you a parable
is only a parable   if it has something
to teach you.

The Story of Icarus,
as Interpreted by J.I.B.

This is everyone's story.   He was born
in a world his father helped build   and
later lived to regret.   So he did his best
to make a pair of wings   hoping Icarus
would be able to stay in the air.   A
lot of my poems are about how people hope
for hopeless things. What is the nature
of tragedy?   Is it that the hero could
have avoided disaster and didn't   or
is it that failure and collapse   were
inevitable   and   the   hero   should   have
never   taken flight in the first place?
Most   parents   followed this   pattern
regret   create   hope   that they
made something that is capable of flying
higher than they could.

This poem is about how   people hope
for hopeless things.

The Truth of Our Illness

We'd like to believe it's something as
poetic as   the fruit from a tree   or
worms from Pandora's box   but really it's
something very human   and by nature
strictly unmagical.   There's no cure
for it.   No drastic course of action.
There's no solution for   ugliness. I am
alive in the most terminal way.   I am
alive with a desire for beautiful and
impossible things. This desire is innate
and unfulfilled and   therefore desperate.
Some people will tell you this   desire
stems from the need for God.   Some people
will tell you   God is dead.   I will tell
you that all the   fruit I eat comes from
a tin can   and we're all full of worms.
Not literally   but nearly so.

The Creation of Something, a Point to All This

The universe is much too big for just one
creation story. God must have killed himself
for us   several times.   On the cross.
As a corpse.   A lot of dismantling.
As an egg.   Shattered.   An ocean of yolk.
A lot of mess.   Almost impossible to
make sense of. We like to tell ourselves
stories/We'll tell ourselves anything. A
sinless man. A people made from dirt and
from bone   to praise and be loved/to be
abused.   Sacrificed. To be made an example
of. To be taught a lesson.   To be freed
from all of life's miracles.   A flood. A
promise. A point to all this. A bunch of
busted glass.   A jar of worms.   Fruit
from a poisoned tree.   Roads paved with
broken girls. A boy who can fly. Boys turned
into guns. A father who loves His children
enough to burn them alive.   We like to
tell ourselves stories. The universe is
much too big   of a mess for there not
to be someone to clean it up. We'll tell
ourselves anything.   There's a point
to all this.

Five Rules of Building a Bird's Nest

"It will be objected, that birds do not learn to make their nests as man does to build, for a bird will make exactly the same nest as the rest of their species, even if they have never seen one, and it is instinct alone that can enable them to do this… Birds brought up from the egg in cages do not make the characteristic nest of their species, even though the proper materials are supplied to them, and often make no nest at all"

— Alfred R. Wallace

Let ruined things lie. Rule one   things that   don't mend dismantle   everything else. Don't invite   violence. Rule two don't build with roses   and deny that it's a crown of thorns. Rule three   build something   sturdy. Don't   fool yourself. There's no such thing as breaking a fall. Rule four things that don't mend dismantle everything else. That one bears repeating. Rule five   don't build a crown of thorns.

The Obituary of J.I.B.

He died in a plane crash in the mid 90's. ~~It was a spectacular massacre. From a height most people only see in dreams. The ones when you've just entered sleep then suddenly you're falling. The crash site was beautiful. A dismantled airplane. Body parts dressed in flames. A blanket of dead birds swallowed whole.~~ There were no survivors. ~~Sure what parts that could be salvaged were. Eventually he pulled himself back together the best he could but he was left at best incomplete. Struggling to wake up every day and perform his best version of normalcy. That's not survival. That's not living. That's not functional. Unable to touch anything without clinging to it for safety. Squeezing until shatter. Tearing to shreds. He'd say this is him doing his best as if that makes up for it. He should have known something that heavy could never stay in the air.~~ Survived by no one.

How I Learned the World Has
No Concern for Our Safety

The first time I saw something being born it
was a litter of ten kittens. They told me
there was   nothing   more natural   than
giving life. That bodies are designed to
perform this function. During this process
holy and necessary for a species' survival
the mother was   split   in   two. In
horror   I asked why she was transformed
into an open wound. They told me   that
nothing on this planet works how it was
meant to. The father wasted no time. Freed
one of his children of its blood. Another
just died. There was no clear reason. Six
of the remaining eight died because the
mother   slowly mending her two halves
back into one   stopped feeding them.
Nothing on this planet works how it was
meant to. The last two died from drinking
antifreeze.   They   told   me   this wasn't
exactly   natural   just the world's way
of tying up   loose ends.

Congratulations, it's a Boy

By age five   his father was doing his
best to make a man of him. He had unusual
methods:

1. Burrowing both fists into the shoulder
blades   elbows deep (this will teach him
how to eat pain).

2. Sculpting his silhouette to fit some
kind of monster.

3. Transfiguring his hands into shovels by
applying some strange alchemy.

4. Making him dig a hole from his belly
though his chest cavity   carving out
enough room for a punching bag.

5. Trapping the voice box in his fist like
a lighting bug.

6. Tightening his grip until there's no
more space for its glow.

We Shared a Bed of Broken Glass

I used to have a friend who was full of
busted light bulbs. Some I assume
were hereditary (his parents were both
black holes) but others he collected
himself. He treated his anatomy like a
trash bag shoveled in as much dead light
as it could hold. Once I saw him unhinge
his jaw swallow the remains of 100 watts
without flinching. Eventually the pressure
of swallowing made the glass snap turned
his lungs into a series of stab wounds.
Lined the insides with grains of sand. His
skin spouted a garden of shards. Made
everything he touched bleed.

Me as a Burn Victim

He keeps a roof over our heads. Our house
furnished
In smoke stacks.
A fire every night
simmered never
put out.
Logically the roof should have caved in
long before it finally did.
A wife of gasoline.
Children of wicker.
A father who eats raw ceiling. I am a
product of a home
robbed of oxygen.

The Requirements for Mending

My brother. Diagnosed. A critical amount
of rage. A fist. My face. The impact. An
X-RAY. An eye socket.   Broken. A nose.
Bent in half. A concussion.   Confusion.
Difficulty making sense. If it's mending it's
full of pain and in pieces. A diagnosis and
the ache it doesn't soothe. A hungry wolf
who knows he's hungry. What a bone needs to
heal.   Fragmentation.   Time and patience
and pain. Realignment. Sometimes a doctor's
hands.   Re-break the bone. No such thing
as a perfect   fit. Rewinding. Replaying.
On repeat. My brother. A fist. A critical
amount of rage. My face. The impact.
An X-RAY. A photo of my bone trying to
mend. What that requires. Fitting the
pieces together   again. Time and patience
and pain.   To be broken in the first
place. My brother and   rage   and a fist.
A diagnosis.   A wolf being called
a wolf.   No time to heal.   No patience.
Pain. A wolf left unfed.   Impact.   A
fist.   A concussion. An X-RAY. My bones.
Everything in pieces. Difficulty making
sense. Confusion. My brother. A critical
amount of rage. A diagnosis and all the good
it's done. No such thing as healing. Not
without pain. The Requirements for Mending.

Fitting the pieces together   again and again. Sometimes by force. Fragmentation. Realignment. No such thing as a perfect fit. To be broken in the first place. To understand you might be broken again. A willingness to become stronger after. Everytime. Everything. In pieces. Full of pain. The way things begin to mend.

My Mother as a Dead Animal /
Every Day the Rope Gets Tighter

By 40 my mother
a monument of roadkill
nothing besides bleeding
found it impossible to breathe.
This ozone of noise unorchestrated. At 20
she learned to tie a noose. Wore one like
a necklace
of thread
and a handful of pearls.
Surrounded herself with executioners.
Every morning she wakes up a doe
still absent of horns
hooves too fresh to stand on their own.
There's nothing beautiful about this.
Headlight. Calamity. The reeking of iron.
On repeat.

A Young Wife and Mother

Her morning was spent in piss. The man lied
like a trash bag   packed with tin cans
drank beer   spilt ash. Untied   it was
all scattered across the linoleum. She ate
bowls of milk and ceiling   counted the
black dots on the fly paper   hanging
like chandeliers. She put the baby to bed
took a shower   washed the black off her
bare feet   shampooed the maggots   from
her hair   kissed them goodbye   wished
them luck.

How His Mother Taught
Him Shame

She put him in a bathtub   told him he was
full of toxic waste.   In a panic   he
split his stomach wide open   squeezed
tight   asked it to leave   in the voice he
talked to God with. By the time the water
was lukewarm   he bled a landfill. With his
elbow arched like angel wings   he made
his open wound a door frame   hoping the
bath water would wash him out. Afterwards
he painted the living room with bubble
bath and blood   looking for her. She built
his whole body once   and she did it out
of thin air. Surely she can handle these
repairs.

Cascading Failure

Lately I've been mourning   a crash site
a heap of smoke   familiar craters   a
small universe of hot metal.   This is
my brother. He can't keep from falling
apart. Our parents made us both using
the same clumpy method. What else do you
expect?
Our mother   an avalanche of loose nuts
and bolts.
Our father   a sculpture   made of a
pair of wings   probably shot off an
airplane.
Me and my brother   monuments of ruble.
A family of four/A cascading failure.
Everyone's made of the same basic
materials at first. A skeleton of wax.
Bird feathers for soft tissue. The rest
of us comes from whatever machinery
our parents can spare   without
malfunction.
Some of us are left bare   making it
difficult to   walk   and impossible to fly.

Outside a Gas Station,
East Jesus Nowhere, United States

Air   toxic   with the reek of
ethanol
and other people's cigarettes.   A
hoard of faces   tattooed   ugly
sometimes but not often   beautiful.
A man begs   for spare change   or smokes
or a phone call
high on methamphetamines   or maybe gold
spray paint. And just beyond that are the
power lines by the overpass where the
teenagers meet   to smoke and fuck and
tie strays together by their tails with
shoelaces   hang them on the wires   like
dirty   sneakers. And beyond that are
railroad tracks where drunks and children
are regularly mowed over   and popsicle
crucifixes are buried in the mud their
bodies landed in. And maybe bodies isn't
the right word   but what was left of
them   and a lot of that soaks into the
dirt. And beyond that are bars my father's
been kicked out of   and alleys he's been
jumped in. And beyond that is another city
another gas station. Another man trying to
make a phone call. Other cats claw each
other to death on power lines and other
teenagers meet   and   smoke   and
fuck.

Other bars.   Other fathers.
The whole planet over
the air is toxic and the fathers are
drinking too much beer
and the trains are screaming and cats draw
their last breaths.

The Summer of 1998,
Moments Before a Disaster

It's the summer of 1998. I am given a
mason jar. Almost everything is black.
My father hasn't made me bleed yet. He
jokes that the grass is high enough to
disappear in. He smells like Budweiser
but his eyes don't reek of violence. There
are lightning bugs. He grabs one. Smashes
it. Makes his open palm glow. He tells me
that even when their hearts stop beating
the blood is still beautiful. Instead I
decide to capture some. To keep them in one
solid piece. It's the summer of 1998. I
am learning that making something bleed
can never be beautiful. I still don't
want to disappear. It's the summer of
1998. There is my father. He smells like
Budweiser   but hasn't made me bleed
yet.

The Typical American Family
at Dinner Time, Early 21st Century

A dinner table. Instant mashed
potatoes. A mother. Makeup smeared. A
dress stained. She insists that everyone
eats in the same room. This ritual
is supposed to mean something. She
hopes they'll capture something precious
during. A stepfather. He likes to watch
videos of car wrecks or other calamities
or animals eating smaller ones. Pork
chops. Chewy like bubble gum. Salt.
A stain that won't come out. Children.
They're not sure that there's anything
precious anywhere. This ritual is supposed
to mean something.

A Needle and a Safety Pin and
a Ball of Yarn

The sun shined again today and today   I'm
held to the Earth   by a safety pin.   And
I am bruised and I am bloody   and   the
sun shined again today and I didn't ask
it to. And the sun is a ball of yarn. And
it's easier for a camel to fit   through
the eye of a needle than   it is for a
rich man   to enter Heaven.   And the sun
brings us each new day   even if we're
poor   and I am poor   and the sun   is
a ball of yarn slowly unraveling.   And
I am trying to run a thread through   the
eye of a needle   and I am held to the
Earth   by a safety pin   and the safety
pin is bucking   and the safety pin   is
going to come undone.   And I am a body
made almost entirely of untethered fabric.
And it is easier for a camel   to fit
through the eye of a needle   than   it is
for a rich man to enter Heaven   and I am
poor   and I am struggling to be thankful
for the sun   and today the sun shined
again   and again I ran thread through
the eye of a needle and the sunshine feels
like a million bare knuckles on my bruised
and bloody body and   the sun
shined today   and I am trying to

be thankful despite   having not asked
it to.   And I am a body made almost
entirely of untethered fabric   bruised
and bloody and unraveling like the sun.
And the sun shined again today

    and the safety pin   bucked   and the
safety pin
came   u n d o n e   and
I ran a thread through the eye of a
needle   and reattached myself to
the Earth   and do you know how
hard it is to thread a needle   when
you are almost entirely untethered fabric?
and do you know how hard it is   to get
into Heaven?

2011

The year was 2011 and everything felt
upside down
and I was drinking. We were all drinking.

We were drunk. We were too young for our
insides to be so dirty. I was drinking and
drunk and young and I hated myself and
I took too many muscle relaxers and my
insides were dirty. Almost dirt. I couldn't
feel my arms or legs. I was getting my dick
sucked and I didn't want my dick sucked and
the girl who was sucking my dick was young
and drinking and drunk and hated herself.
Our insides were dirty. Our insides were
almost dirt. We didn't want to be dirt but
we didn't know how to be anything else. We
were too young to hate ourselves like we
did. I was young. I was drinking. I had
taken too many muscle relaxers. I was drunk
and I hated myself. I was sinking. The
floorboards. The foundation of the house.
The top soil. I was drunk and I took too
many muscle relaxers. I was drunk and I
couldn't feel my arms and legs and I was
sinking. I was sinking. The floorboards.
The foundation of the house. The topsoil.
Below the topsoil. I couldn't feel my arms

and legs. I couldn't feel my arms and legs.
All I could feel was dirt. I was sinking. I
was sinking. I was young and I was drinking
and I was drunk and I was falling asleep.
I was falling asleep and I wasn't sure if
I was going to wake up. Everything was
upside down.

The year was 2011.

Note on Freudian Psychology, the Summer of 2013

My mother and I spent the summer of 2013 destroying bridges in my grandma's apartment. We never cleaned up this wreckage. In fact we made furniture out of it. I slept on a bed of raw infrastructure. Ate bowls of milk and ceiling. I used to think it was a skill creating out of damage. Freud got one thing wrong about the Oedipus complex. It isn't that we want to fuck our mothers it's that a craftsman is more comfortable working with familiar parts.

A Hot Car, 2019

The Earth   is a lot hotter   than it's
supposed to be.   The A/C is broken. My
mother says that it doesn't   make sense.
It shouldn't be   broken   today. It worked
yesterday.   Yesterday we told each other
the truth   again. The truth is   rarely
innocent. The Earth   is   a lot hotter
than it's supposed to be. People who   are
considered experts on the subject say that
it's   too late   to save ourselves.
I almost tell her *That's the nature of
broken things. One day they work. One day
they don't.*   But that isn't the truth.
The truth   is almost always more brutal.
Brutality takes time.   Things don't just
break.   Things are broken.   Today we're
talking to each other like   everything is
still in one   solid piece. Yesterday we
told each other   the truth.

Frankenstein's Monster, 1999

I spent a lot of that year terrified.
You made that easy. Your body like
Frankenstein's monster. Made of various
parts. Sown together and horrific. Only
vaguely human. Most nights I tried to
sleep under the sound of you grunting
and growling and throwing the little
girl in the water. You never considered
whether or not she could swim.   She
couldn't. Most nights I slept while
my mother was drowning. Choking river
water   on flower petals plucked. I spent
a lot of that year drawing pictures of
you. No one else was suited for the job.
More than anyone I knew the edges of your
horror show. Your hands   designed for
strangulation. The inside of your skull
a slaughter house. Your chest cavity
packed with a black mass that's always
screaming and frightening everything that
sees it.   Sometimes the Devil in
your belly. An unholy thing.
 What else do you expect from a thing
  created so   u n n a t u r a l l y?

A Summary of a Movie I Want to Make, Semi-Autobiographical

I want to make a movie about a man in mourning. His brother. A dead body. Lungs. Bloated. Leaking suicide. It'll start with a series of establishing shots. Maybe in black and white. A bird torn. Almost down to its basic parts. A pair of hands. Wearing something else's blood and belonging to a child. In the movie the man wears the suit he wore to his brother's funeral every day. And when he passes a dead bird on the street he shoves it in a hole he dug in his chest. This movie won't shy away from magical realism. This movie will have no real plot. No resolution or lesson learned. His brother dropped from a window. A note left behind. Something about the impossibility of flight. While mourning the man dug the hole in his chest the one I told you about earlier. He buried the birds in it because they reminded him of the time his brother learned that making something bleed can never be beautiful. Eventually the man had to remove his innards to make room for grave sites. Vital organs useless. Stuffed with feathers and bits of beak and bone. By the second act the man finds a way to use the

41

parts   recovered. Pieced the birds back
together   bit by bit by bit.   Once
they're in one solid piece   he tosses
them from the same window   his brother
dropped out   of   to see if they'll take
flight. And because it's a movie   they do.
But this movie will ultimately be   more
interested in the world as it is   rather
than the world as we'd like to make it.
The narrator will tell the audience that
the beautiful thing about movies is   a
filmmaker can chop and shape and rearrange
everything. Have it all make sense. By the
third act   the man will break the fourth
wall.   Will reverse the   reel. Frame
by frame by frame.   All the way back to
the   establishing shots. Do everything in
technicolor.   Show his brother how to put
the bird back together.   Teach him that
blood is ugly without exception. Watch
the bird fly away.   Fade to black. Then the
narrator will tell the audience that life
is not like a movie.   That this wasn't
based on true events. That nothing makes
any sense.

That the world is not beautiful.

The Impossibility of Mending

I write a lot about impossible things.
For instance   in this poem I'm writing
about a plate of glass.   I will state that
every plate of glass crafted will   almost
certainly shatter eventually. When the one
I'm writing about finally does   it'll be
shoved in a box   and asked to put itself
back together.   See.   Impossible. In
this poem   I'll tell you that we daydream
because   the world is not beautiful. I
want to write a children's book. It'll
be about   a box full of broken glass.
Divine intervention will make   it come to
life. Grow arms and legs.   The box
lives in   a world that is not beautiful
because everyone in it   is missing
parts. So the box goes to find its creator
hoping He will grant the parts required
to function   properly. But when the box
finds the creator   He's   every bit as
incomplete   as everyone else.   The moral
of the story isn't a moral. The moral of
the story is a reminder that if we're made
in God's image   maybe he's   uglier
than we allow ourselves to believe.   So
anyways there's a plate of glass.   Every
plate of glass will   almost   certainly
shatter eventually. When this one finally

did   it was packed in a box. Told to get
itself back to one solid piece. Actually
there were many plates of glass. Actually
there are   too many to count.   One
Box.   No results.   We daydream because
the world is not beautiful.

So He Made a Scrapbook

She managed to love a pile of broken
glass. Got used to treating her arms
like shovels. Cradled the shards like
a newborn. Laid it out along the kitchen
table. Spent hours sorting through
them like puzzle pieces. Didn't sleep
until they formed a functioning baby boy.
When she finished his reconstruction
his skull was full of Polaroids of her
licking her split fingertips.

Song of My Mother

It is a music I have given up on
naming. Like a car crash. Like a box
of broken glass rattling. Tiny broken
things that in just the right light
might glow but will ultimately make
you bleed. Sung in the same voice she used
to tell God to go fuck Himself. I can no
longer believe in a God that didn't scream
back. I no longer pretend I'm listening to
jazz and that it'll all make sense at
the end and it'll be beautiful.

The Ugliness of Bird Cages

It's innate. As it would be for anything designed to capture something beautiful enough to have the option not to touch the Earth. They're carefully crafted. Mimic harps. Or more fittingly spider webs. They ought to be jagged. A box made of crucifixes. A sculpture of a grenade in the middle of detonation. A rib cage forced completely shut. Something that says *You won't leave this place alive.* Something that says *If this doesn't keep you from taking flight I will clip your feathers.*

Photographs

Time as we know it doesn't exist.
Literally speaking   time is   we are
here covering this   patch of empty
space
now we are here   covering
this one. They say the universe is
expanding.   I believe this is an
optimistic interpretation. Everything
is falling   in the same direction.
Everything is falling at an increasing
speed. We invented photography.
We snapped light into a fragment
clipped its feathers   so it could
never fly away. With it we can capture
the instant that leaves struggling
against a thunderstorm are still. Or
the moment before a bird lands and
it's motionless
but manages to stay in the air   as if
it belongs there. We do this to fool
ourselves into thinking it's possible
to take flight

            and never touch the ground again.

January 23rd, 2018,
Moments Before a Disaster

It's January   23rd   2018. I am not
dressed   in gasoline   and you're not
dripping with suicide and we both believe
in Heaven   figure we were born   there
together   and   later   forcibly   removed.
It's January   23rd   2018. We spent
the month   taking pictures of angels and
naming children   we haven't drowned yet.
It's January   23rd   2018.   For a while
I'm a good person
not a fucking house fire   and for a while
you aren't a reminder that the world is
mired in people who never asked to be born.
It's January   23rd   2018. The pictures
we're taking are just headlights   passed
by on the highway.

Note on Modern Infrastructure

Birds are creatures of instinct.
When faced with the chaos of architecture
they build nests in power lines.
This is an ugly miracle.
Making a home in a body with such
potential
to destroy.
To convert feathers into fireworks.
You are a creature of suicidal ideations.
You are sharing a bed with me.
Like my father before me I am a house
fire. Eventually I will swallow
everything.
Drink all the oxygen.
Love the resulting ashes.
Apologize   as if it makes up for it.

The Science of Human Sacrifice

I've performed self-mutilation
even made a ritual out of it.
I consider this ritual beautiful.
The way I slaughter   making room for a
whole person   to crawl in   to feed on.
Without this I am hungry.
I imagine this is what it's like to be a
mother   or an incubator
(we all start as something
 between a parasite and a miracle). I
admit I'm no expert on human biology
but I've seen enough to know our species
often needs to make something
incomplete to feel whole.

Jeffery Dahmer, Serial Killer

"The only motivation there ever was, complete control of a person. A person I found physically attractive. Keep them with me as long as possible. Even if that meant just keeping a part of them." — Jeffry Dahmer

We all need beautiful things. They are as essential   to us as the   frontal cortex the spinal column   the four chambers of the human heart   anything that without we cannot   function   as we're meant to.   We can't imagine the hideousness of the absence of something like the   circulatory system. Not only the   resulting blood   but the horror of new   empty   space.   We all need beautiful things   to stay.   When they leave   we all become guilty of eating without concern for what our teeth tear apart   of dissecting   whatever we find miraculous   of clinging   to the parts we love the most   of attempting to fill in all this absence.   This is intimacy. By the end we have our   subjects in a way no one else does   and they know us like no other living thing possibly can.

Things I Don't Consider
Self Destructive

Loving things   that want to eat me
alive.   Confusing   intimacy   with
letting them do it.   Committing my violence
when I'm alone.   Always being alone
when   I'm   committing   my   violence.
Talking to God   again.   Telling Him
to go fuck Himself in the same voice my
mother used. Thinking about all the people
ruined   along the way.   Their broken
pieces.   The ones still inside my body.
Pulling them out   until I'm exhausted.
Until my fingers are bleeding. Ignoring my
bleeding. Bleeding all the fucking time.
Becoming an exit wound.
Loving other exit wounds.   Then stabbing
each other to death.
Effortlessly and without ceasing.

Inherent Destruction

I came back to town thinking I was a
pilgrim   or maybe a refugee   but
I was a voodoo doll. A cursed thing
like my father before me. I suffer
from loose seams. I ruined myself
with needle pricks. It wasn't self-
mutilation.
There was something in my feathers.
Trapped beneath my fabric. Something
digging. Alien   I hope. I managed
to pluck some of it out.   Among the
parasites gathered was   toxic
waste
a few of the worms that slithered
from Pandora's box   an infant free
of oxygen   more than a few birds
dead. But no matter how much of it
I removed   there was always more.
I carried this collection with me.
Held them to my chest as if they were
my children   or exposed and vital
organs.   Then offered them up   like
communion bread   to anyone I saw
saying *please   take   they're too
heavy for one set of arms.* I came
into town thinking I was a pilgrim
full of famine and illness   or
maybe a refugee   a person venerable

and without home. I came back to town
falling to pieces like my father before
me. I've made a habit of it.

You as a Detonated Grenade

I dug you out of me with a railroad
spike. Any graceful instrument wouldn't
have been fitting. I needed something
rusted for this. Shrapnel. Designed to
not necessarily kill the victim but
 to make them wish it had been. I
dug you out. I needed something that
would splinter my skull. Once it did I
started pulling you out. Whole handfuls
like carving a pumpkin. The more of
you I shoveled out   the more I found
hiding beneath.
I titled this poem *You as a Detonated
Grenade* because any graceful title
wouldn't have been fitting. You were
something too loud to ignore. Something
that for an instant   swallowed up
everything in the most destructive way
imaginable.
You didn't kill me but for a while I
was hollowed out.

The Creation of Something, an Ugly Miracle

When I asked where I came from you
told me that you and my father asked
an old man in outer space permission
to make a baby boy. He said   *yes.*
Turned your hands into shovels   your
torso into topsoil.   Told you to start
digging to find all your   best parts
to   remove them   then start
building.   That wasn't the truth.
The truth is never   so lovely. I was
made with   what   you had to spare.
Harp strings   clipped. Porcelain
dolls   dismantled.   A belly full of
toxic waste. Broken glass in a box reading
JIGSAW PUZZLE.   A hornet's nest for
a skull. Do you remember how in the
beginning of Frankenstein   the Doctor
thought he had built something miraculous
but by the end he was ready to let it
all   burn   to the ground? Saying I
was made from what   you had to spare
is not entirely accurate. I was made
from what you had left.   I hope
there's enough in me to make something
functional.   I can be a lot of things.
A Jigsaw puzzle.   I can be
broken glass. A house fire.   I can be

Frankenstein's monster.   I can be ugly.
A miracle. But I can't be someone who
creates   something just to watch it
burn. I want to   rewind   the   movie
all   the   way back to the beginning when
the Doctor still believed in miracles.
Pause.   Remove the tape.   When my child
asks where they came from   I will tell
them we asked an old man in outer space
for a baby. He said *yes* and sent one down.
I had nothing to do with construction.

A Poem About the Baby Bird
I Helped Kill

~~We are damage from the same plane~~
~~crash. Spent a lot of time falling and~~
~~clinging to each other. Two separate~~
~~components hoping our bond would~~
~~soften the shock of hitting the ground.~~
~~I never let you look away. I never let~~
~~you think the black dots were ants. No.~~
~~They were wreckage that had already~~
~~made their craters. I told you I was~~
~~surprised the dying bird we came from~~
~~ever got off the ground in the first~~
~~place. I wish I had let you close~~
~~your eyes. Maybe you would have fallen~~
~~asleep thought we turned into blue~~
~~jays starting flying.~~

I'm tempted to compare our parents to
engine failure   but they were just
two   dysfunctional   people   performing
their best version of normalcy. We were
not a cascading failure. We were two
kids sharing a bed in a house too loud
to sleep in. I wrote this trying   to
apologize for things I barely understand.
When you were four you killed a baby
bird. I let you know it was your fault

59

that it would never fly. You'd tell me
I'm wrong   but I know you resent me. I
want to speak frankly to you about this
but I keep wanting   to use figurative
language. It's a coping mechanism. I try
to make everything beautiful. I taught
you about suicide and that God was dead.
There's nothing beautiful about that. I
wrote this because I want to say I love
you and I'm sorry and fuck you for not
forgiving me. Let's be honest   we were
never anything   poetic   like flowers
or parts of a combusted airplane. I want
to say something like *we share the same
wound*   and *where one wound ends   the
other begins*. I like that   but that's
not the truth. But it's not far from it.

Witnessing a Beautiful Thing

You are a small universe of light
bulbs   shaped like a human body. I
don't understand how you move   without
shattering   or how you touch anything
without it catching fire. And when I see
you   I think about how   in a perfect
world   I would wake up in your bed
the next morning. Sometimes I live in a
perfect world.   Sometimes I wake up
in a small universe full of electricity
without fear of electrocution. Somehow
I touch you without   being afraid of
burning my palms   or breaking glass.

The Divinity of Architecture

I helped make a human life. This isn't
something people should be able to do
by accident. I've never been able to
create anything functional. In fact
the opposite is true. I am an architect of
broken things rearranged functionally
but free of loveliness. I like to think
there's an art to this. In hiding it all
inside myself. Not unlike Pandora's box.
I always thought it would be better if
I weren't opened up. I helped make a
human life. A beautiful accident. When
I tell the mother that she has a small
universe of beautiful things inside her
all worthy of giving a child she says
So do you. I hope she's right. I hope
to find every little piece. I hope to
give them until there's nothing left.

Note on a Dream, A Crash Dummy

In a dream I was falling   from a
height that only   exists in   sleep.
Maybe I stepped off some cliff   on some
far-off planet. I was   too terrified to
breathe. Sometimes it's impossible   to
breathe anywhere   even when your feet
are steady.   All I know for certain
is   where there once was solid ground
there was a sudden absence. The ground
didn't   say goodbye   or even give
warning.   It didn't wait   to see if I
landed   safely. Nothing does after   it
decides to disappear.   I flapped my arms
pretended I   was an airplane. I think it
worked for a minute   or   at least I
fooled myself into thinking I was starting
to take flight.   But eventually I came to
terms with   it   got comfortable with
cascading. Finally   when I   hit bottom
I realized I was made to survive impact.

The Possibility of Flight

There was a veil of snow over the whole city so fragile that I destroyed it a little with every step I took. There's something absent about walking down a street without a sidewalk. Ears lose the blistering of automobiles. In this silence I begin to disappear. In this silence I am nothing but my footprints. In this silence I daydream that I'm a bird. I theorize that the only way to live without dismantling things is to grow feathers take flight and never land. I theorize a lot about this and other impossibilities. I crossed paths with an airplane trying to find someplace to land. That it hadn't crashed yet was an ugly miracle. I theorize it's impossible to land without collision. As a kid I wondered what planes ate. I figured it was birds that the sound they make comes from beaks getting trapped in their windpipes. Of course they're big enough to eat anything. Maybe even the sky. I theorize that if they come down any faster they might shatter the baby blue like a windshield and when the dust finally settled there

~~wouldn't be anywhere left to take off.~~
~~I theorize that human beings like~~
~~airplanes are capable of spectacular~~
~~disaster but under the right conditions~~
we can fly.

Listening to Music in Utero

Listen.   I'm trying   to give you
something   urgently.   My most
beautiful thing.   Maybe my only thing
worth giving.   It's something like a
love note. Only language   is too weak
for this.   Nothing I could say would
ever be true   enough. I haven't had it
long.   In fact   it's just now sprouted
from my dirt. Despite having never been
watered.   Something from nothing. By
definition a miracle   can never be ugly.
Somehow you planted the seed of it in
me   deeper than I thought possible.
Deeper than the human body should allow.
Before you were born.   Before you had
hands to dig with. By definition a miracle
can never be ugly.   That bears repeating
Listen.   The music will have to do for
now. I'm trying my best   to dig it all
up for you   but even the instruments are
failing us. Nothing on this planet works
the way it's meant to. In English the best
translation I have to offer is   *I loved
you before you had a brain in your skull.*
Those are the truest words I've found
so   far.

A Shower, An Acid Trip, New Year's Eve, 2019

I was baptized before this.   A tub of
cold water.   The hands of a stranger.
I was a child who miraculously never
shed any skin.   Just collected it.   A
hideous   thing. The kind of ugliness
that you'd assume must have started
in the womb. I don't know exactly why
I brought you here. Why I stripped us
naked. You a carefully crafted statue
depicting fertility. Me the same ghastly
collection of flesh.   Maybe I was hoping
this time the water would leak in
through to my bones.   Maybe you'd peel
me as if I were a tree. As if you could
physically dig   through every year of
my life. Remove the moment I decided
I don't deserve to be happy. Carve the
rest into the shape of the statue of
Venus with the arms still   intact. And
maybe this time she will stay complete
and beautiful.   Instead you split
your   torso open.   Had me crawl in.
For a moment   you were   carrying
more than one child. For a moment   I
was inside you   patiently waiting to
be reborn.

The Pile of Dust We Will Give You the Day You're Born

It will be all we have to offer you.
A mess. Mostly human skin   and
other things reduced to their smallest
possible parts. This place has a way of
doing that. Of smashing everything it's
given. You are no exception. You will
certainly be demolished. Reassembled.
You will shed several layers of flesh. We
are bringing you here because we still
believe we can make something beautiful
out of it. All this dust. I will sit
in it with you   make sand castles
that will enviably topple under their
own weight. We'll build it back up.
I won't regret this.

I am a Carpenter's Son

I cannot call this moment miraculous.
A room full of iron. Your mother
unzipped and leaking. You   simply and
naturally a pile of clay.   Bloody and
formless. No. I am no sculptor   but
I am trying.   Maybe against all
possibility   to keep you in one
solid piece. This requires both hands.
This requires   dexterity   that I
do not possess.   But I am trying.
God damn. I am trying   to craft
something   capable of flight. I am
trying to craft a body   irises stuffed
with Heaven   a head rattling with harp
stings fully intact   hands capable
of transforming me   having already
turned to stone.

If Things Don't Mend,
What Do They Do?

Things   that   don't   mend   dismantle
everything else.
Things   that don't mend   what do
they do?
Dismantle.   Things
dismantle things.
If they don't mend. Things that don't
mend   dismantle.   Things that don't
mend dismantle.   Things   don't
mend.
Things dismantle things. Things dismantle
things. Dismantle things. Things dismantle
things.   Things   dismantle.   Things.
Dismantle. What do things do? Dismantle.
Things. Dismantle. Dismantle. What else?
Dismantle everything. Everything else.
Dismantle   everything   else.   Dismantle
everything   what else? If they don't
mend. what do they do? Dismantle.
what else? If they don't mend   what else
do they do? What else do they do? What
else? Dismantle.   What do they
do if they don't   mend?   dismantle
everything else. Things dismantle.
Things dismantle
everything else.   Everything.

Dismantle.   Everything.
Dismantle.   Everything.
Everything   dismantle.
Things that don't mend
dismantle   everything   else.
Things   that   mend   don't.
Things that mend don't   dismantle.
Things that mend don't.   Dismantle.
Things that mend don't.   Things that
mend don't dismantle. Things   mend
don't   dismantle.   Things   mend.
Don't dismantle. Things mend   don't
dismantle.   Things   that   mend   don't
dismantle. Things that mend   don't
dismantle. Things mend. Things mend.
Things   mend.   Things.   Mend.   Don't
dismantle. Things mend.
Don't dismantle.

The Creation of Something, Test Swan

God's first swan was not beautiful   but
like the planet   it   was   born   on
a twisted   jagged form.   Could hardly
be understood   as a single organism.
Feathers   combustible   and   poorly
attached to skin   still bleeding   from
its clumsy   assembly.   A scrap metal
skeleton   much too heavy to ever
truly fly. Maybe this was never meant to
be the finished product.   A test swan.
A work in progress.
Or maybe God was not the craftsman He
thought He was.
During its first attempt at flight   the
moment before disaster   was the happiest
God had ever been.
He picked up the pieces. Rebuilt what
amounted to a smoldering husk.   Applied
bandages   reattached feathers with
Elmer's glue.   The test swan was told
to try   again.
That it needed to learn from its failure.
Told to stand up straighter   to stretch
its wings
beyond   the limit   of its design.
Several failures later. Nothing learned.
So the test swan began the slow and painful

process of becoming beautiful. Removing
most   of its skeleton.   Beating its
ribs into   the shape of a bird cage.
Ignoring bloodshed.
Eventually   the test swan   managed
to stay in the air
and it never landed.

Covering a Patch of Empty Space

I am here   now   and that's good.

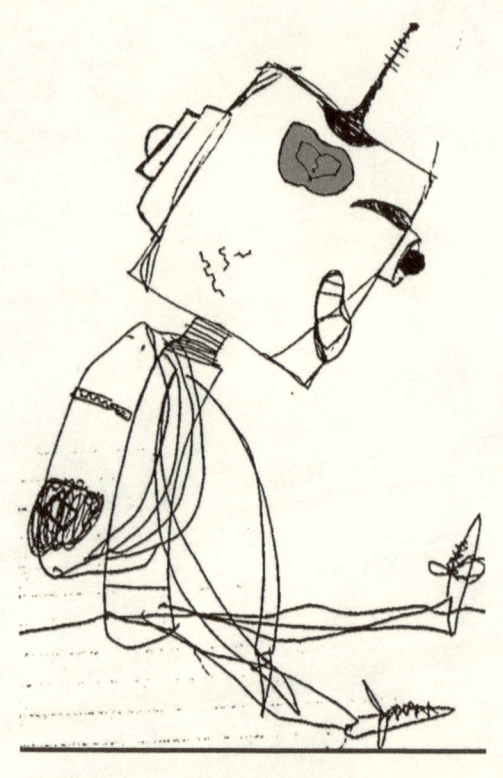

Acknowledgments

"Notes on Modern Infrastructure" appeared in **All The Sins,** November 2019

An earlier version of "Smothered" and the poem "A Young Wife and Mother" appeared in the chapbook *Route 23 to Golgotha,* (EMP, 2019

"So He Made a Chapbook" appeared in **Recap,** Spring 2019

"We Shared a Bed of Broken Glass", "Smothered", "Congratulations, it's a Boy", and "Lightening Bugs in a Mason Jar" appeared in **Deep Overstock,** July 2020.

"A Shower, an Acid Trip, New Years Eve 2019" appeared in **All the Sins,** June 2020.

J.I.B. is a prose poet from Southern Ohio. His work has been published with journals, magazines, and various midwest presses, including EMP. You can follow his work, travels and performances on **instagram @j.i.b.trash.poet**.

www.ingramcontent.com/pod-product-compliance
Lightning Source LLC
Chambersburg PA
CBHW030510130626
46549CB00007B/2925